This book is a collaboration between
Fondation Ipsen and Mayo Clinic.

The story has been inspired by
Golden Ella's experience with sickle cell disease.

The words in bold refer to key terms on page 32.

MEDICAL EDITOR

Asmaa Ferdjallah, M.D., M.P.H., Senior Associate Consultant, Division of Pediatric
Hematology/Oncology, Mayo Clinic, Rochester, MN; Assistant Professor of Pediatrics,
Mayo Clinic College of Medicine and Science

SERIES CONCEPTION

Fredric B. Meyer, M.D., Consultant, Department of Neurologic Surgery, Mayo Clinic,
Rochester, MN; Executive Dean of Education, Professor of Neurosurgery,
Mayo Clinic College of Medicine and Science

James A. Levine, M.D., Ph.D., Professor, President, Fondation Ipsen, Paris, France

My Life Beyond
SICKLE CELL DISEASE

A Mayo Clinic patient story
by Hey Gee and Golden Ella

MAYO CLINIC PRESS KIDS

Foreword

Hi!

My name is Golden Ella, and sickle cell disease has been a part of my life since I was 9 months old. I was already walking, and my mom and dad say I was a chubby-cheeked, curious, lively, smart and friendly baby girl. Suddenly, I became very ill, with a lot of pain in my hips and joints. I stopped walking and was listless, on my back, not able to even lift my arms and legs. I went to the emergency room and was hospitalized. I had osteomyelitis, an infection of the hipbones. That's when we found out I have sickle cell disease.
My hipbone infection was a complication of the disease. I had surgery and several infusions, and unending clinic and hospital visits. It was a revolving door.

However, I, for one, have decided sickle cell disease should not stop me from being my vivacious, vibrant and versatile self! I am a dancer and a Lego robotics programmer, builder and competitor. I like coding and computer programming. I am in drama and honors choir too. I sing my heart out! And I run track and field, holding my own even when I tire easily. I am doing my best to live life to its fullest potential. I hope to become a pediatric hematologist/ oncologist, like the specialist doctor I see, and find a cure for sickle cell disease.

As you read this book, I hope you find the courage to lift yourself up and live your life to its fullest potential. If you have sickle cell disease, it does not need to define your amazing future. Stay positive! Be your vivacious, versatile and can-do self. Wishing you a healthful life journey.

Peace, love and health,
Golden Ella

NOTHING IS
IMPOSSIBLE

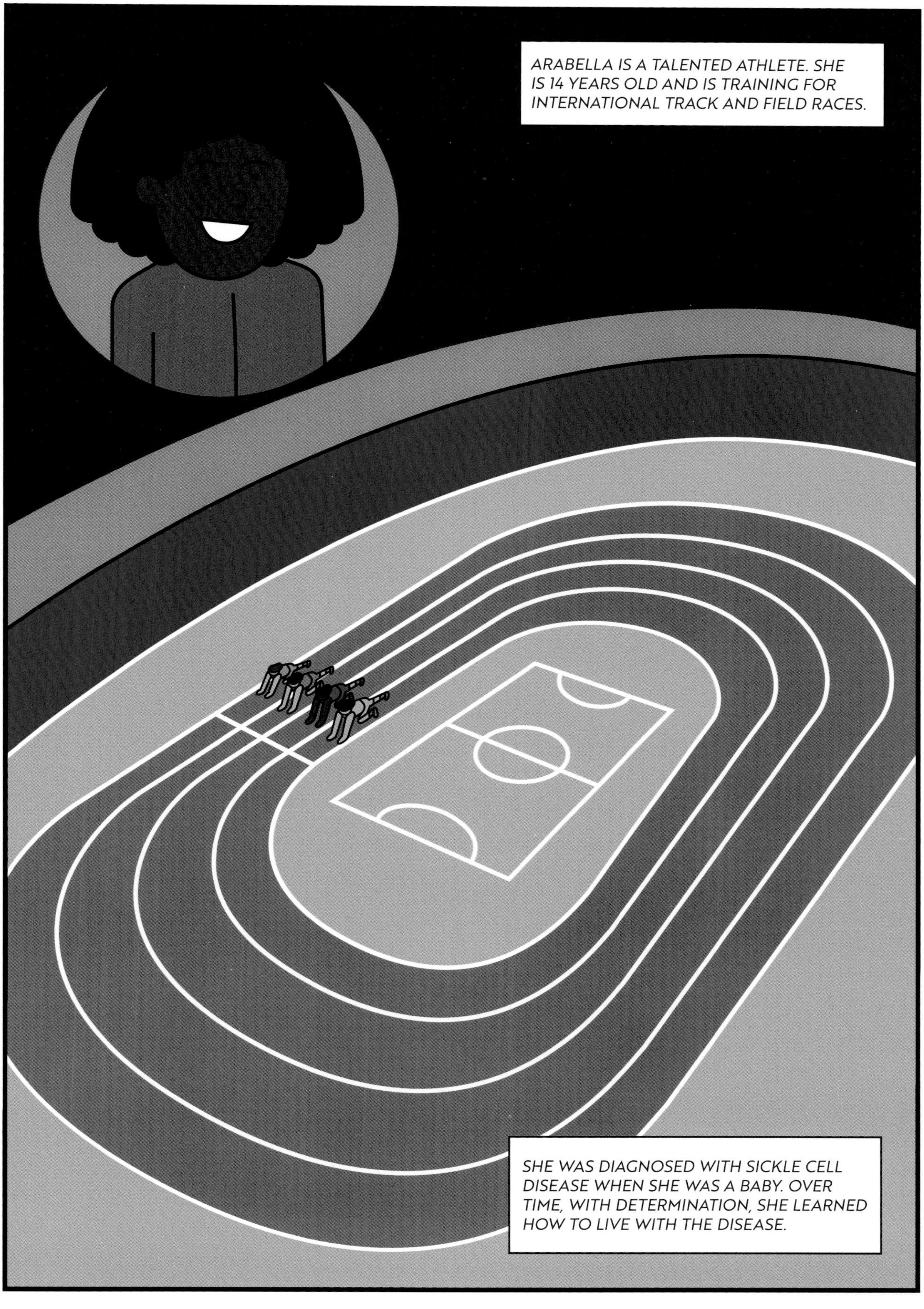
ARABELLA IS A TALENTED ATHLETE. SHE IS 14 YEARS OLD AND IS TRAINING FOR INTERNATIONAL TRACK AND FIELD RACES.
SHE WAS DIAGNOSED WITH SICKLE CELL DISEASE WHEN SHE WAS A BABY. OVER TIME, WITH DETERMINATION, SHE LEARNED HOW TO LIVE WITH THE DISEASE.

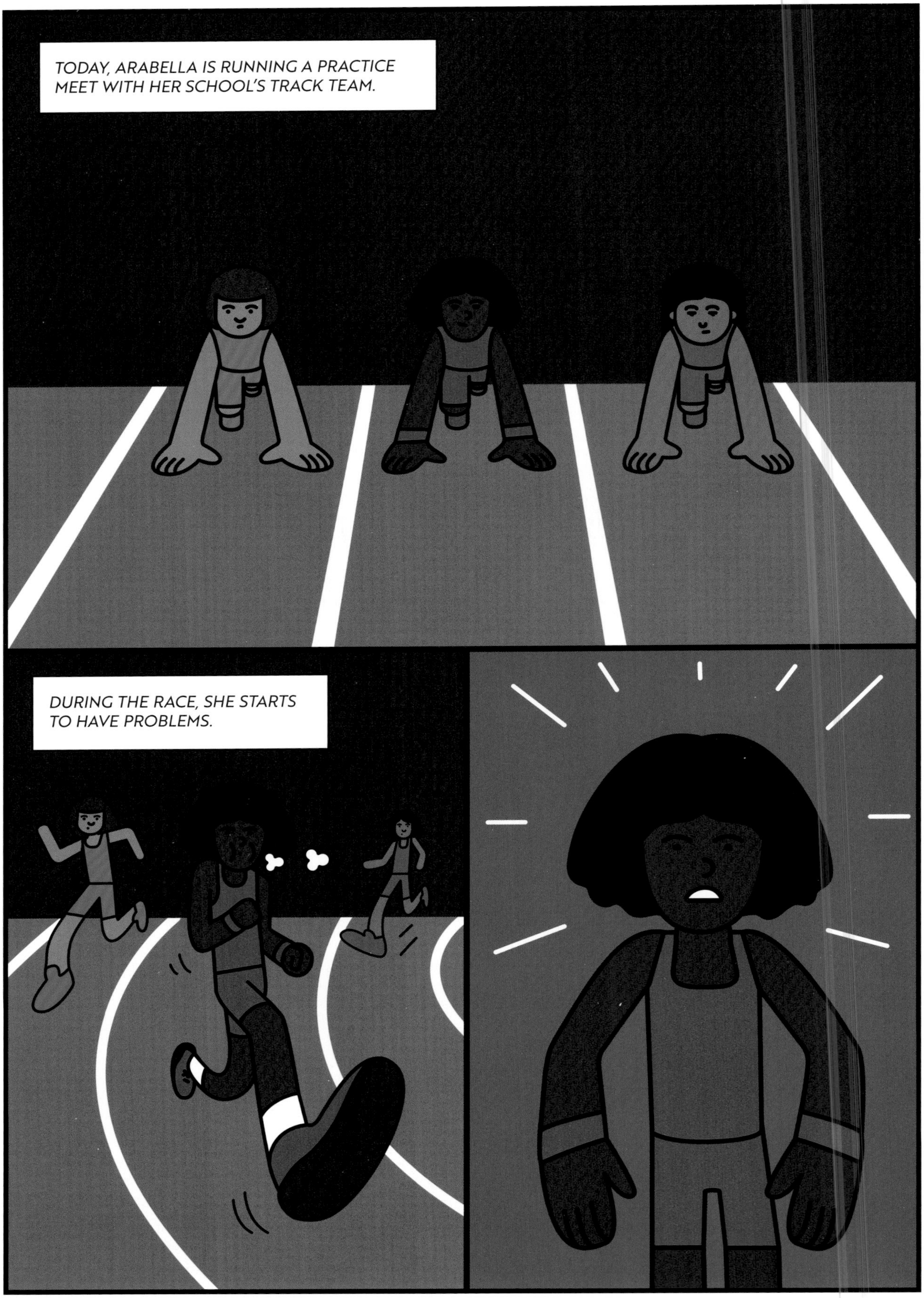
TODAY, ARABELLA IS RUNNING A PRACTICE MEET WITH HER SCHOOL'S TRACK TEAM.
DURING THE RACE, SHE STARTS TO HAVE PROBLEMS.

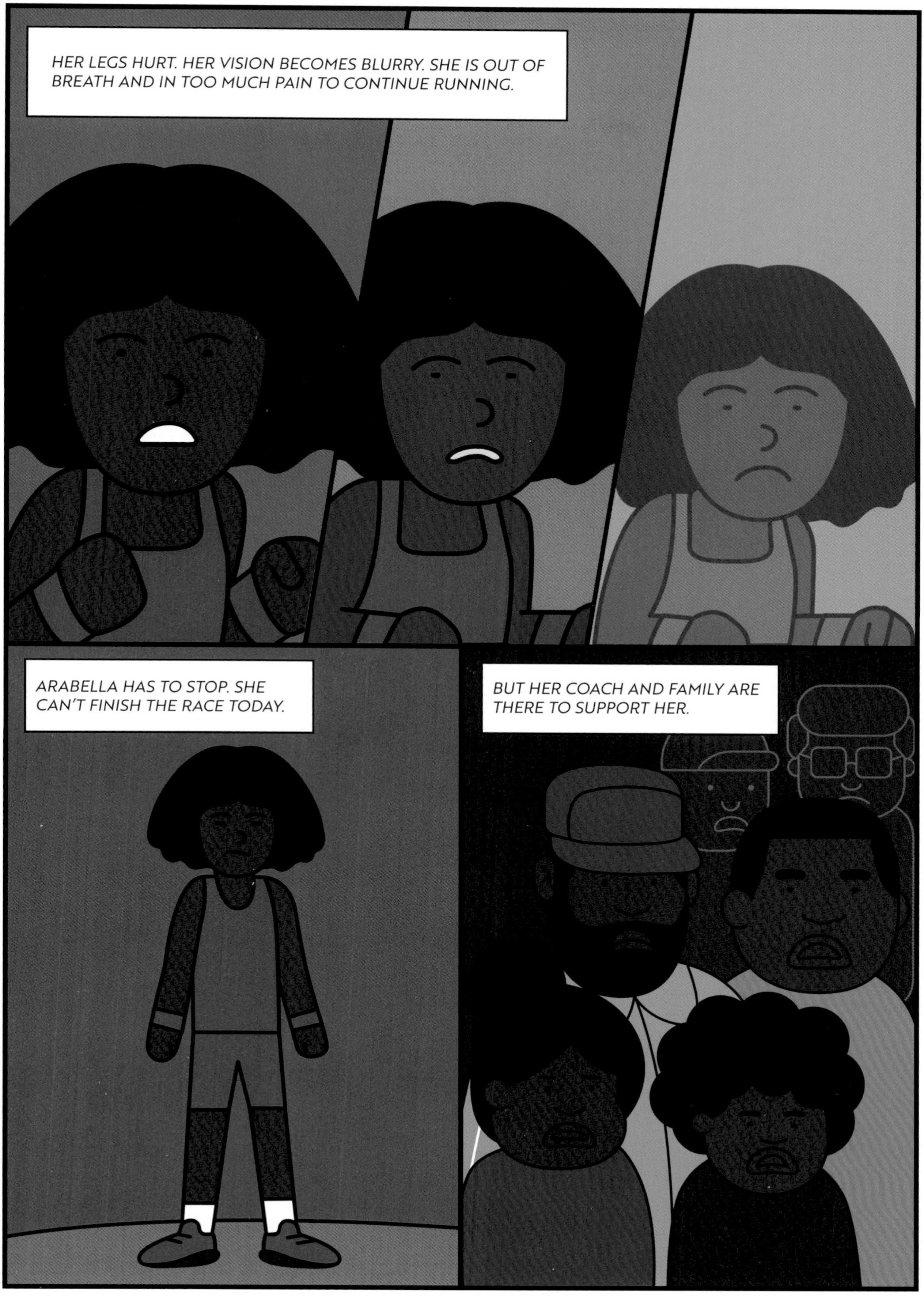
HER LEGS HURT. HER VISION BECOMES BLURRY. SHE IS OUT OF BREATH AND IN TOO MUCH PAIN TO CONTINUE RUNNING.
ARABELLA HAS TO STOP. SHE CAN'T FINISH THE RACE TODAY.
BUT HER COACH AND FAMILY ARE THERE TO SUPPORT HER.

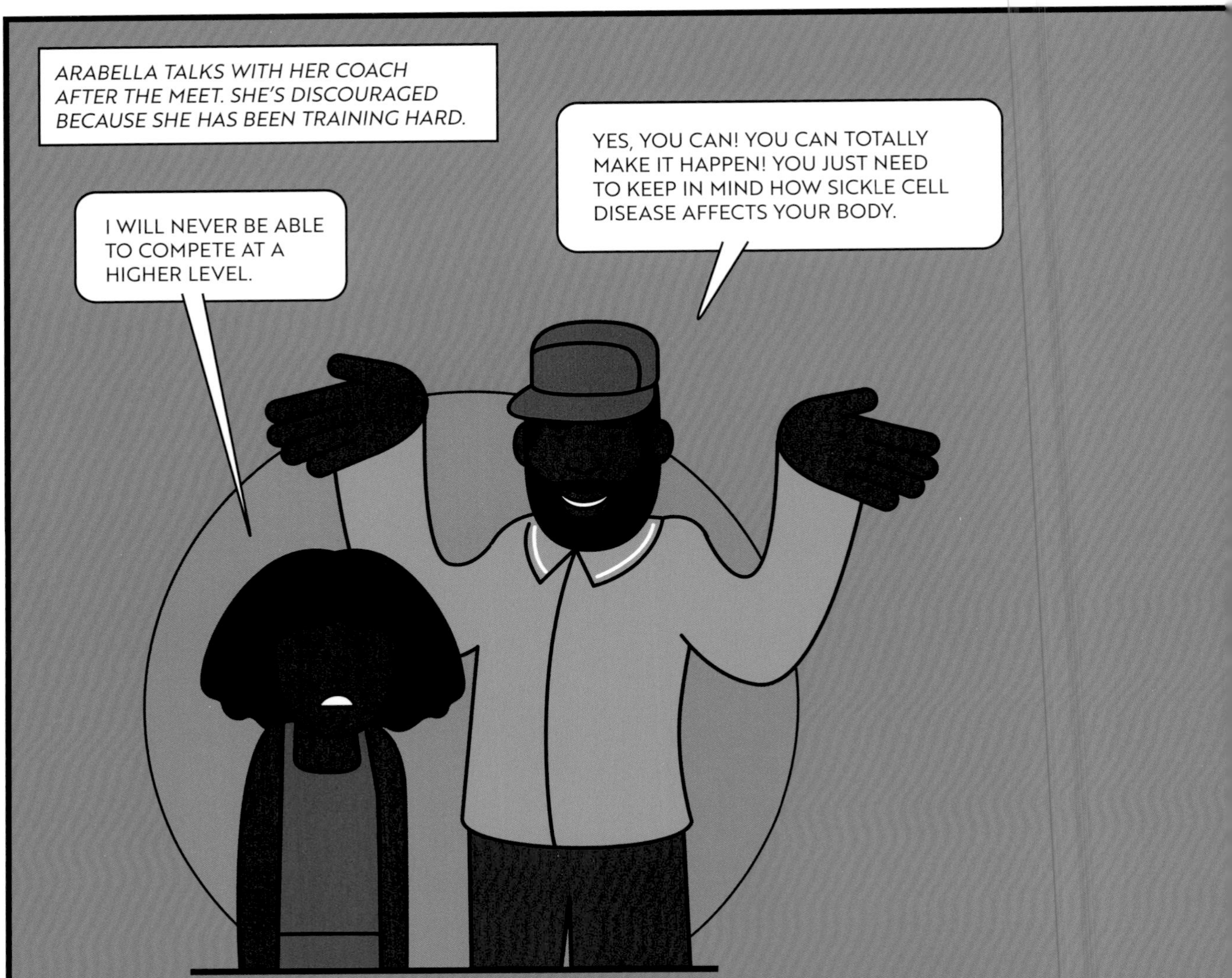
ARABELLA TALKS WITH HER COACH AFTER THE MEET. SHE'S DISCOURAGED BECAUSE SHE HAS BEEN TRAINING HARD.
I WILL NEVER BE ABLE TO COMPETE AT A HIGHER LEVEL.
YES, YOU CAN! YOU CAN TOTALLY MAKE IT HAPPEN! YOU JUST NEED TO KEEP IN MIND HOW SICKLE CELL DISEASE AFFECTS YOUR BODY.

ABOUT SICKLE CELL DISEASE

*SICKLE CELL DISEASE AFFECTS **RED BLOOD CELLS** THAT CARRY OXYGEN THROUGHOUT THE BODY. HEALTHY **RED BLOOD CELLS** ARE ROUND AND FLEXIBLE. BUT WITH SICKLE CELL DISEASE, SOME OF THESE CELLS BECOME STIFF AND STICKY AND SHAPED LIKE CRESCENT MOONS, ALSO CALLED SICKLE-SHAPED.*

THEY EASILY GET STUCK IN SMALL BLOOD VESSELS. THIS CAN SLOW OR BLOCK THE FLOW OF BLOOD AND OXYGEN AROUND THE BODY.

*SICKLE CELL DISEASE CAUSES **ANEMIA**. **ANEMIA** IS WHEN A PERSON DOES NOT HAVE ENOUGH HEALTHY **RED BLOOD CELLS** TO CARRY OXYGEN THROUGHOUT THE BODY. **ANEMIA** CAN CAUSE TIMES OF EXTREME PAIN CALLED PAIN CRISES.*

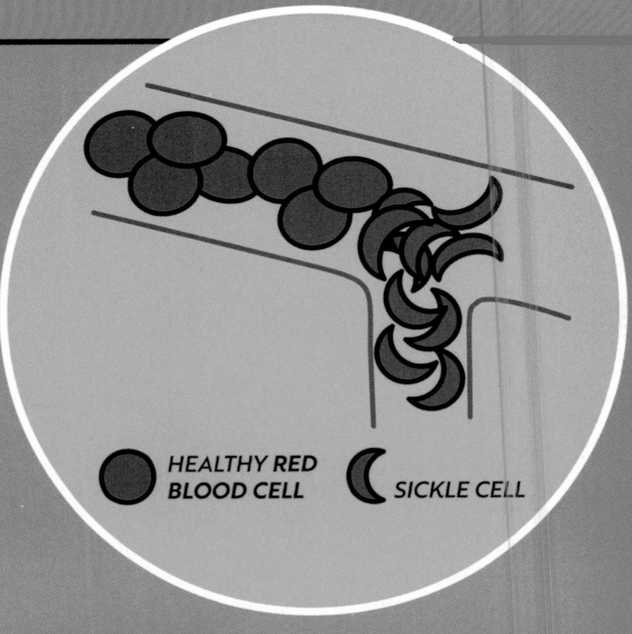
HEALTHY RED BLOOD CELL
SICKLE CELL

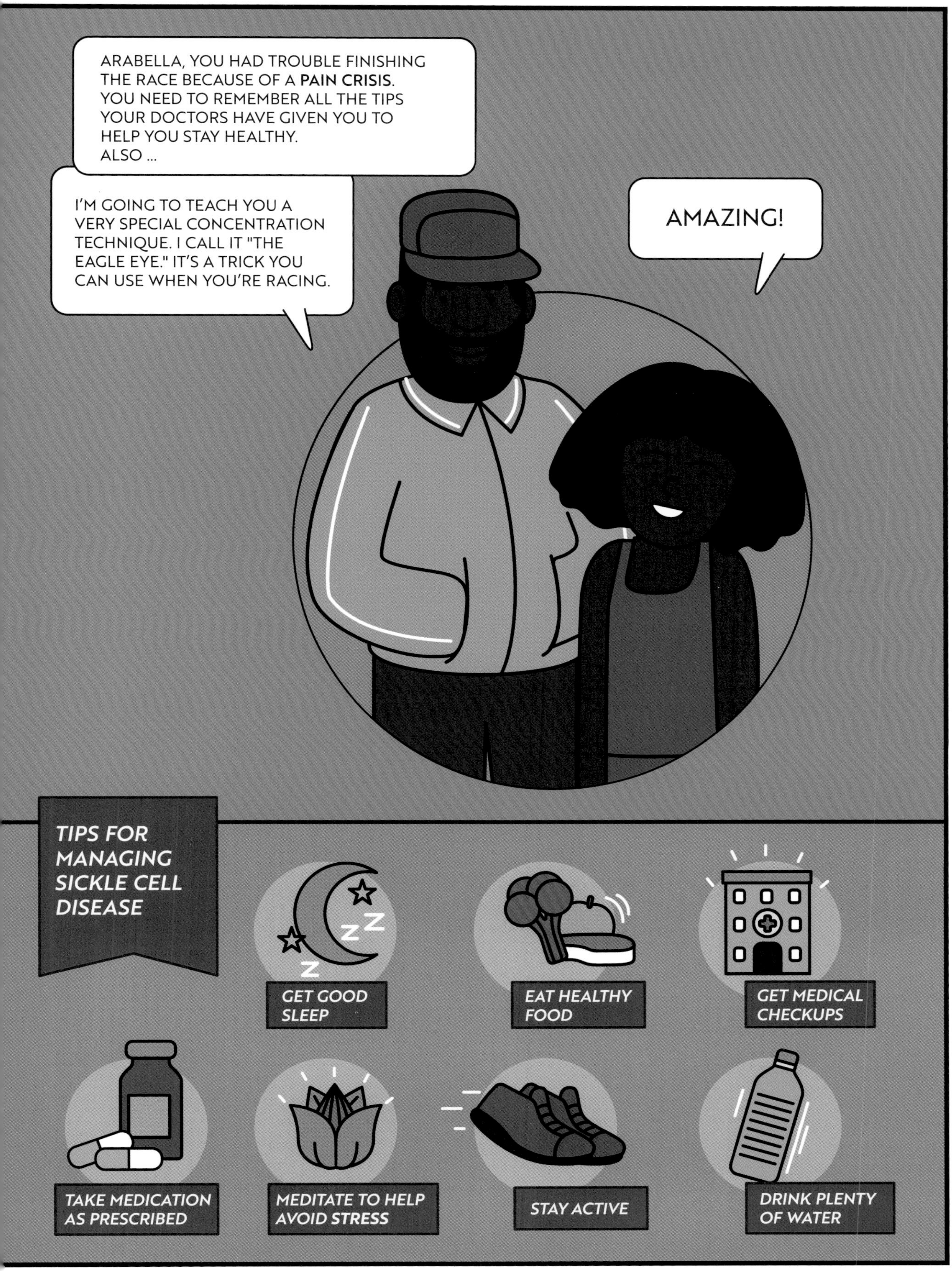

ARABELLA, YOU HAD TROUBLE FINISHING THE RACE BECAUSE OF A **PAIN CRISIS**. YOU NEED TO REMEMBER ALL THE TIPS YOUR DOCTORS HAVE GIVEN YOU TO HELP YOU STAY HEALTHY. ALSO ...

I'M GOING TO TEACH YOU A VERY SPECIAL CONCENTRATION TECHNIQUE. I CALL IT "THE EAGLE EYE." IT'S A TRICK YOU CAN USE WHEN YOU'RE RACING.

AMAZING!

TIPS FOR MANAGING SICKLE CELL DISEASE

GET GOOD SLEEP

EAT HEALTHY FOOD

GET MEDICAL CHECKUPS

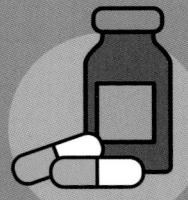

TAKE MEDICATION AS PRESCRIBED

MEDITATE TO HELP AVOID **STRESS**

STAY ACTIVE

DRINK PLENTY OF WATER

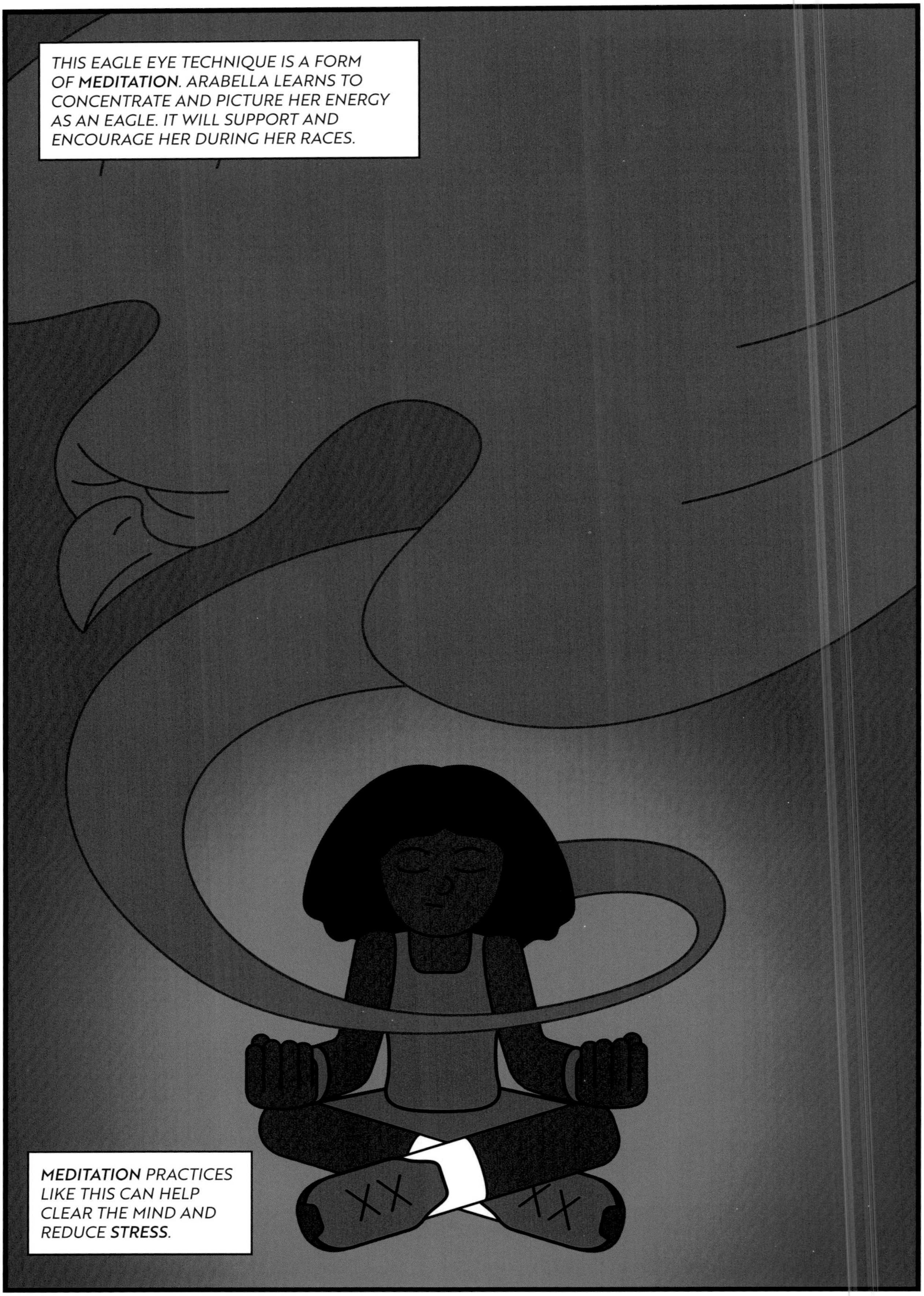
THIS EAGLE EYE TECHNIQUE IS A FORM OF **MEDITATION**. ARABELLA LEARNS TO CONCENTRATE AND PICTURE HER ENERGY AS AN EAGLE. IT WILL SUPPORT AND ENCOURAGE HER DURING HER RACES.
MEDITATION PRACTICES LIKE THIS CAN HELP CLEAR THE MIND AND REDUCE **STRESS**.

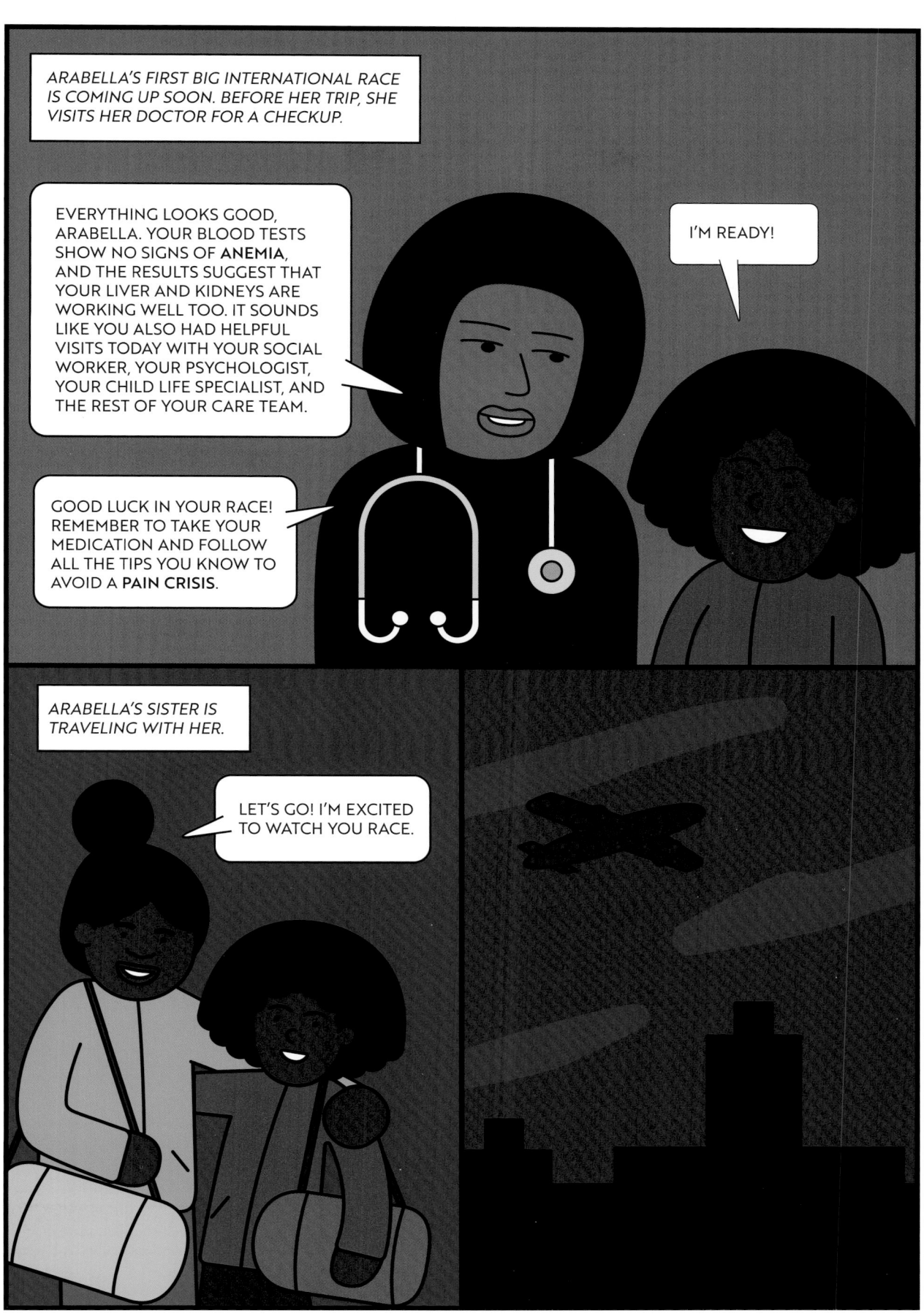

ARABELLA'S FIRST BIG INTERNATIONAL RACE IS COMING UP SOON. BEFORE HER TRIP, SHE VISITS HER DOCTOR FOR A CHECKUP.

EVERYTHING LOOKS GOOD, ARABELLA. YOUR BLOOD TESTS SHOW NO SIGNS OF **ANEMIA**, AND THE RESULTS SUGGEST THAT YOUR LIVER AND KIDNEYS ARE WORKING WELL TOO. IT SOUNDS LIKE YOU ALSO HAD HELPFUL VISITS TODAY WITH YOUR SOCIAL WORKER, YOUR PSYCHOLOGIST, YOUR CHILD LIFE SPECIALIST, AND THE REST OF YOUR CARE TEAM.

I'M READY!

GOOD LUCK IN YOUR RACE! REMEMBER TO TAKE YOUR MEDICATION AND FOLLOW ALL THE TIPS YOU KNOW TO AVOID A **PAIN CRISIS**.

ARABELLA'S SISTER IS TRAVELING WITH HER.

LET'S GO! I'M EXCITED TO WATCH YOU RACE.

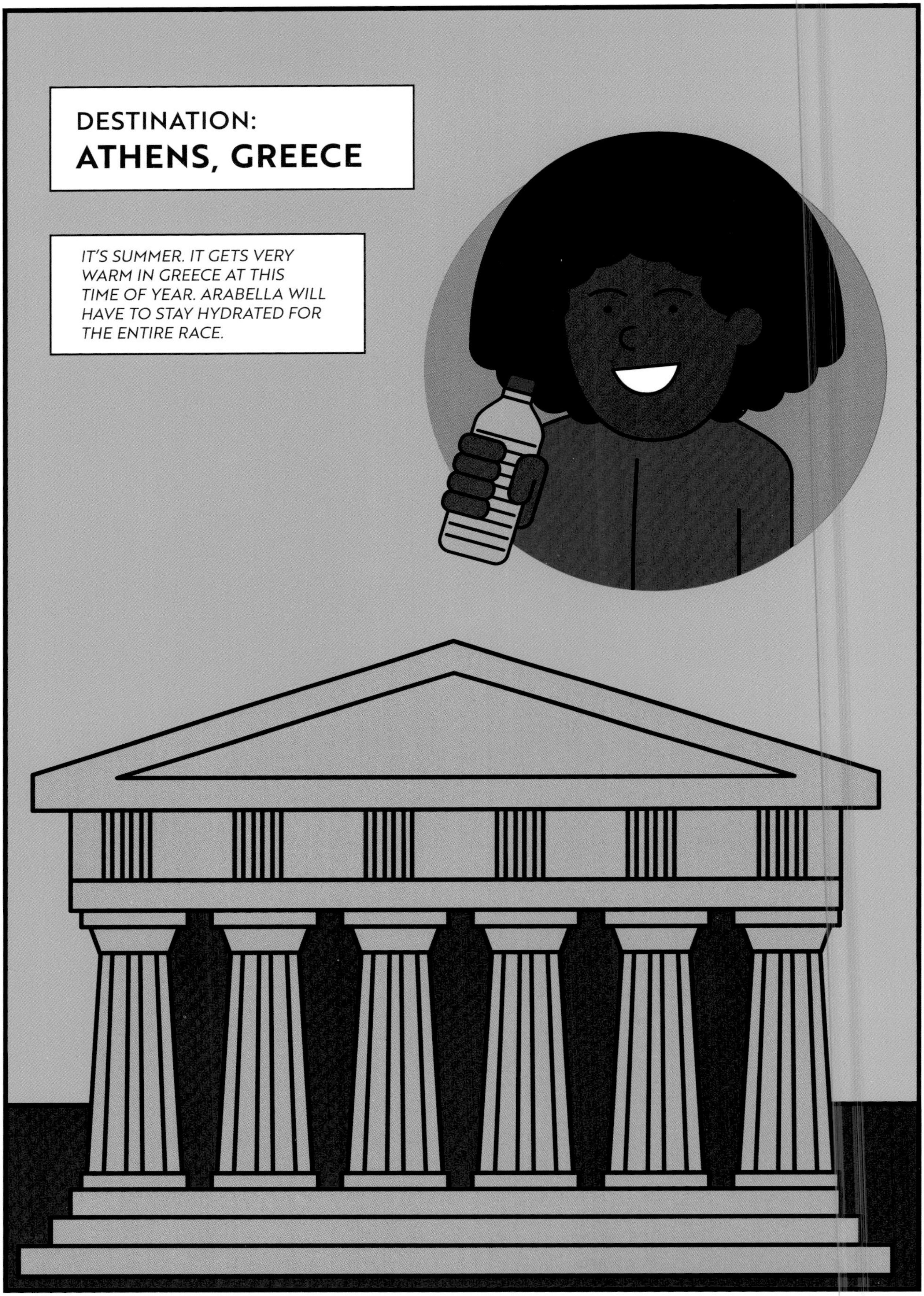
DESTINATION:
ATHENS, GREECE
IT'S SUMMER. IT GETS VERY WARM IN GREECE AT THIS TIME OF YEAR. ARABELLA WILL HAVE TO STAY HYDRATED FOR THE ENTIRE RACE.

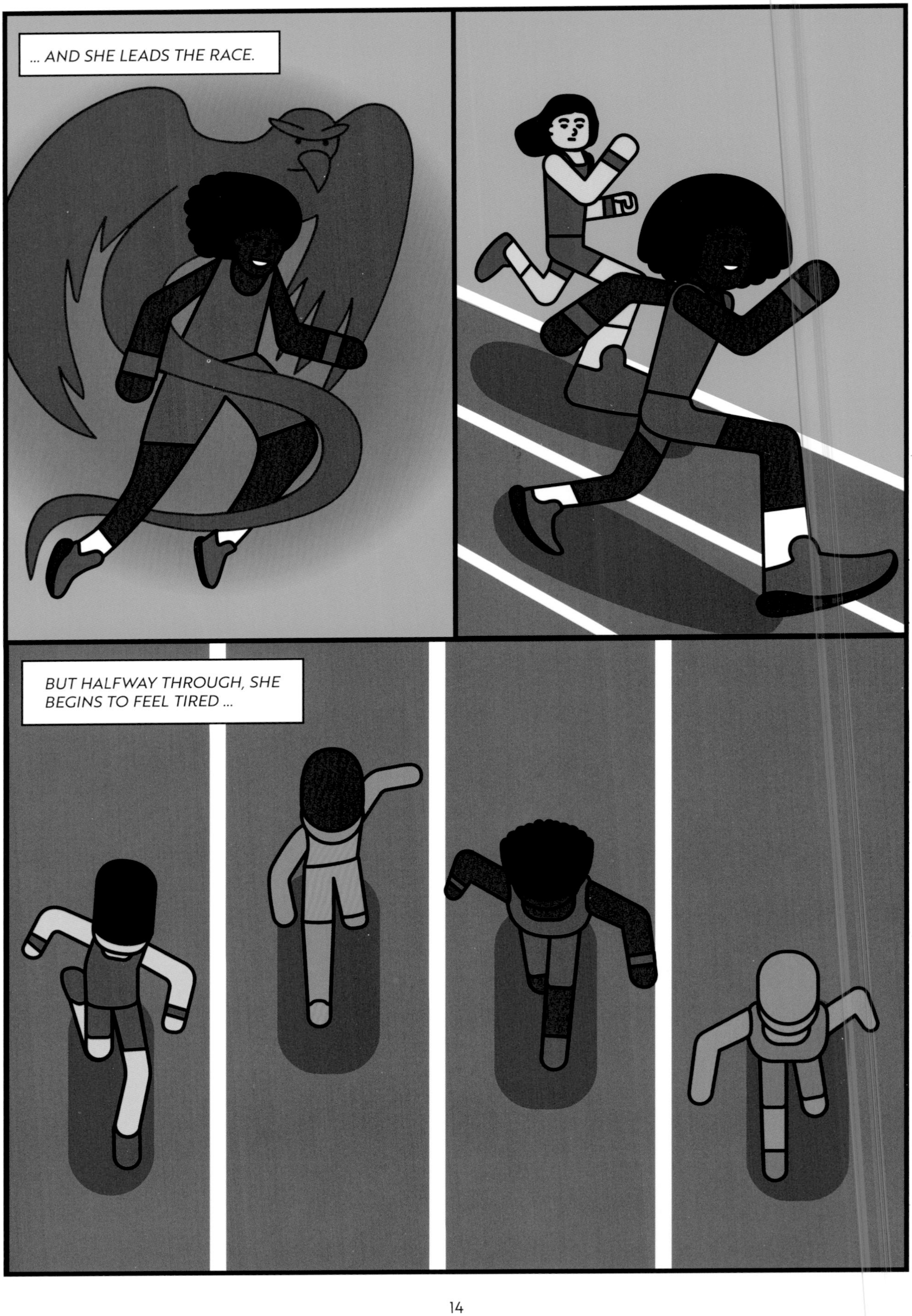
... AND SHE LEADS THE RACE.
BUT HALFWAY THROUGH, SHE BEGINS TO FEEL TIRED ...

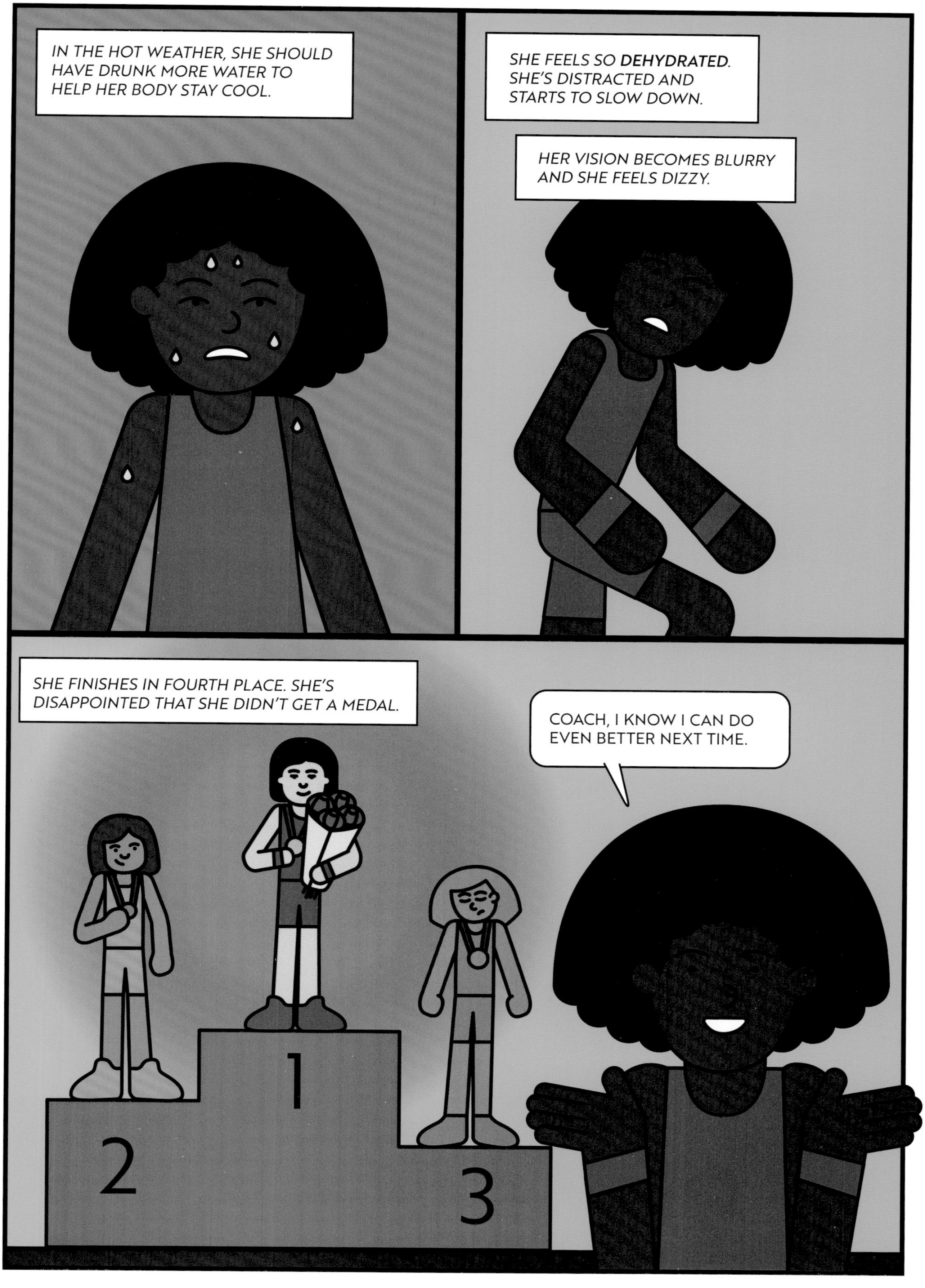
IN THE HOT WEATHER, SHE SHOULD HAVE DRUNK MORE WATER TO HELP HER BODY STAY COOL.
SHE FEELS SO **DEHYDRATED**. SHE'S DISTRACTED AND STARTS TO SLOW DOWN.
HER VISION BECOMES BLURRY AND SHE FEELS DIZZY.
SHE FINISHES IN FOURTH PLACE. SHE'S DISAPPOINTED THAT SHE DIDN'T GET A MEDAL.
1
2
3
COACH, I KNOW I CAN DO EVEN BETTER NEXT TIME.

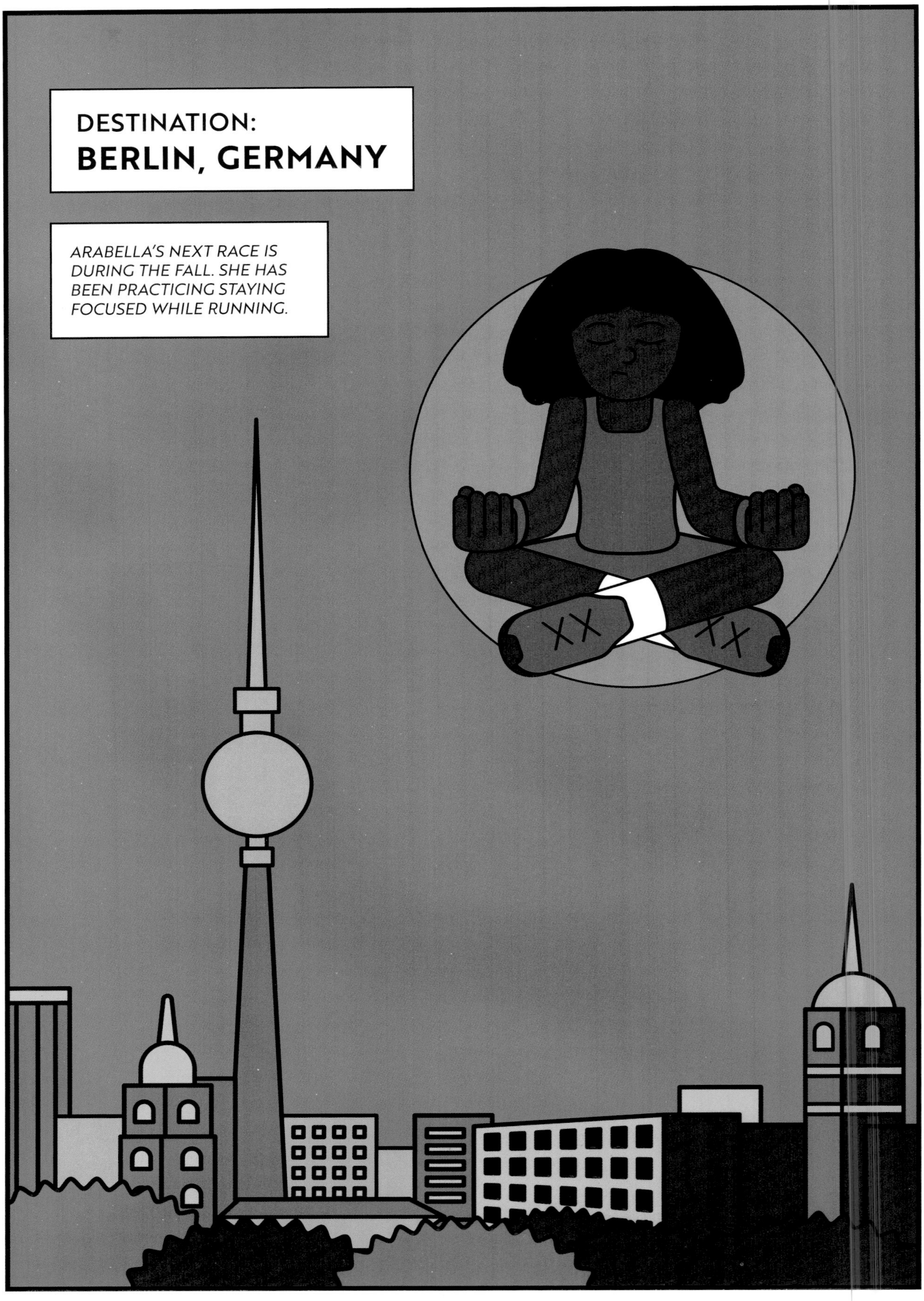
DESTINATION:
BERLIN, GERMANY
ARABELLA'S NEXT RACE IS DURING THE FALL. SHE HAS BEEN PRACTICING STAYING FOCUSED WHILE RUNNING.

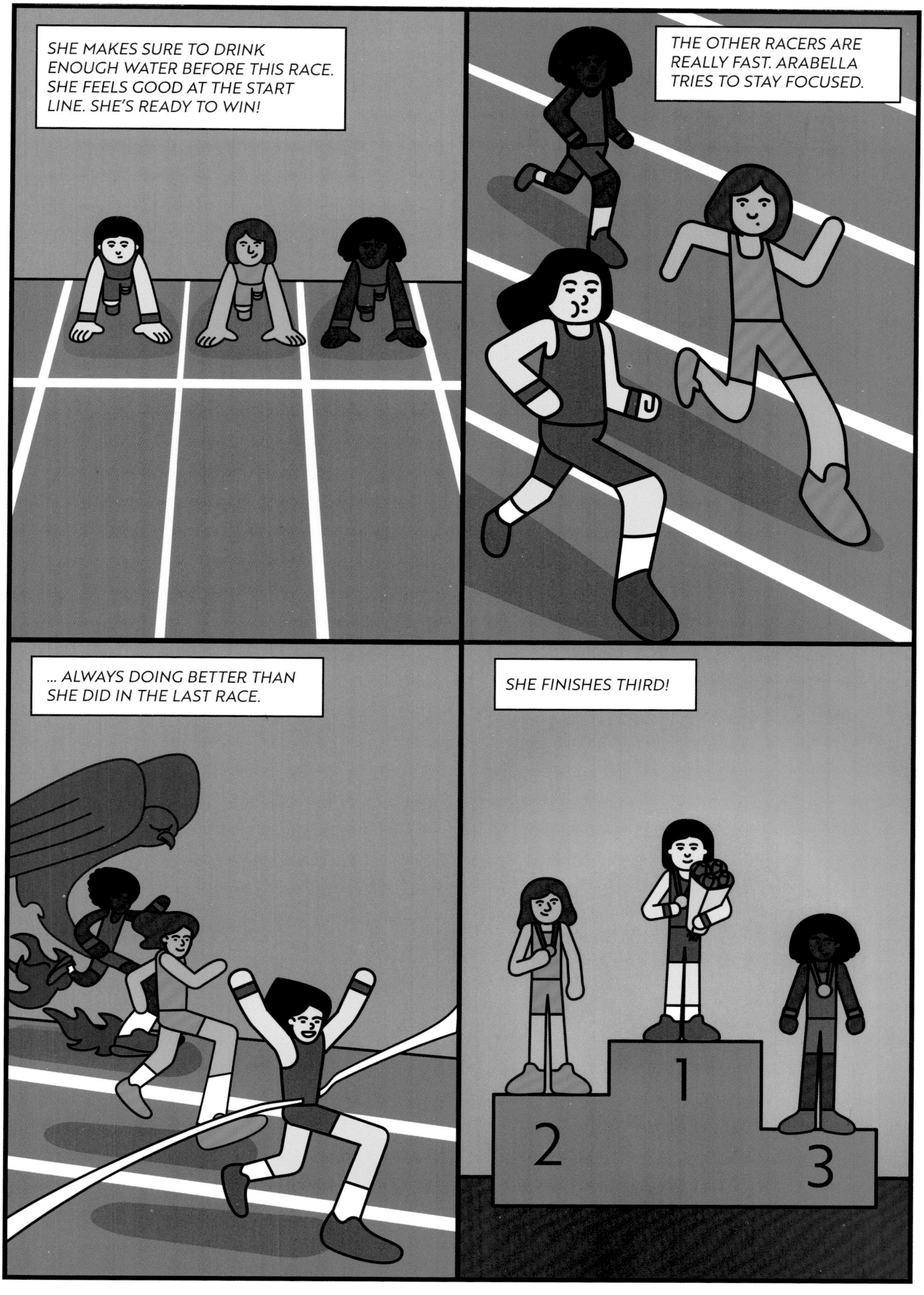
SHE MAKES SURE TO DRINK ENOUGH WATER BEFORE THIS RACE. SHE FEELS GOOD AT THE START LINE. SHE'S READY TO WIN!
THE OTHER RACERS ARE REALLY FAST. ARABELLA TRIES TO STAY FOCUSED.
... ALWAYS DOING BETTER THAN SHE DID IN THE LAST RACE.
SHE FINISHES THIRD!
1
2
3

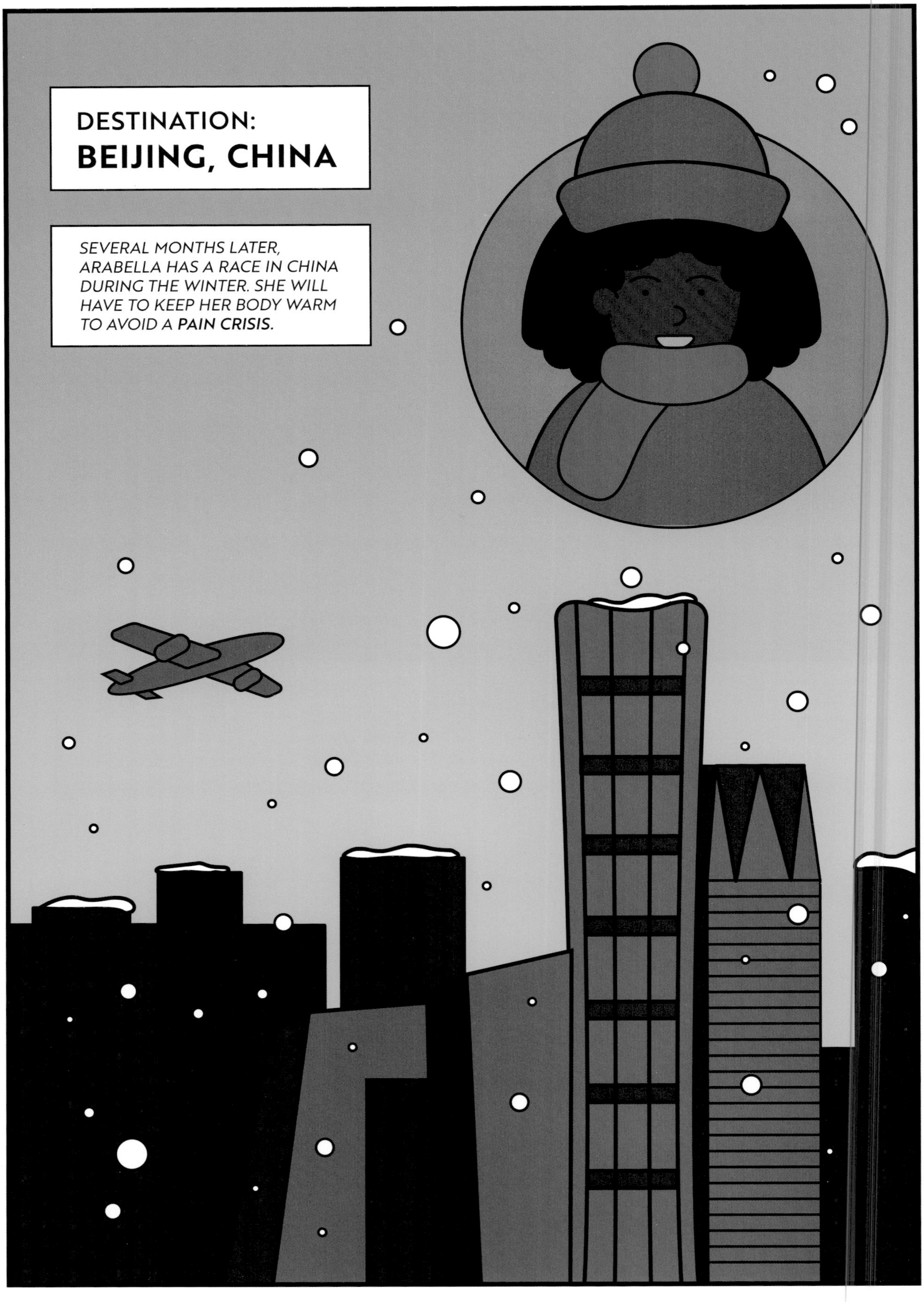
DESTINATION:
BEIJING, CHINA
SEVERAL MONTHS LATER, ARABELLA HAS A RACE IN CHINA DURING THE WINTER. SHE WILL HAVE TO KEEP HER BODY WARM TO AVOID A **PAIN CRISIS.**

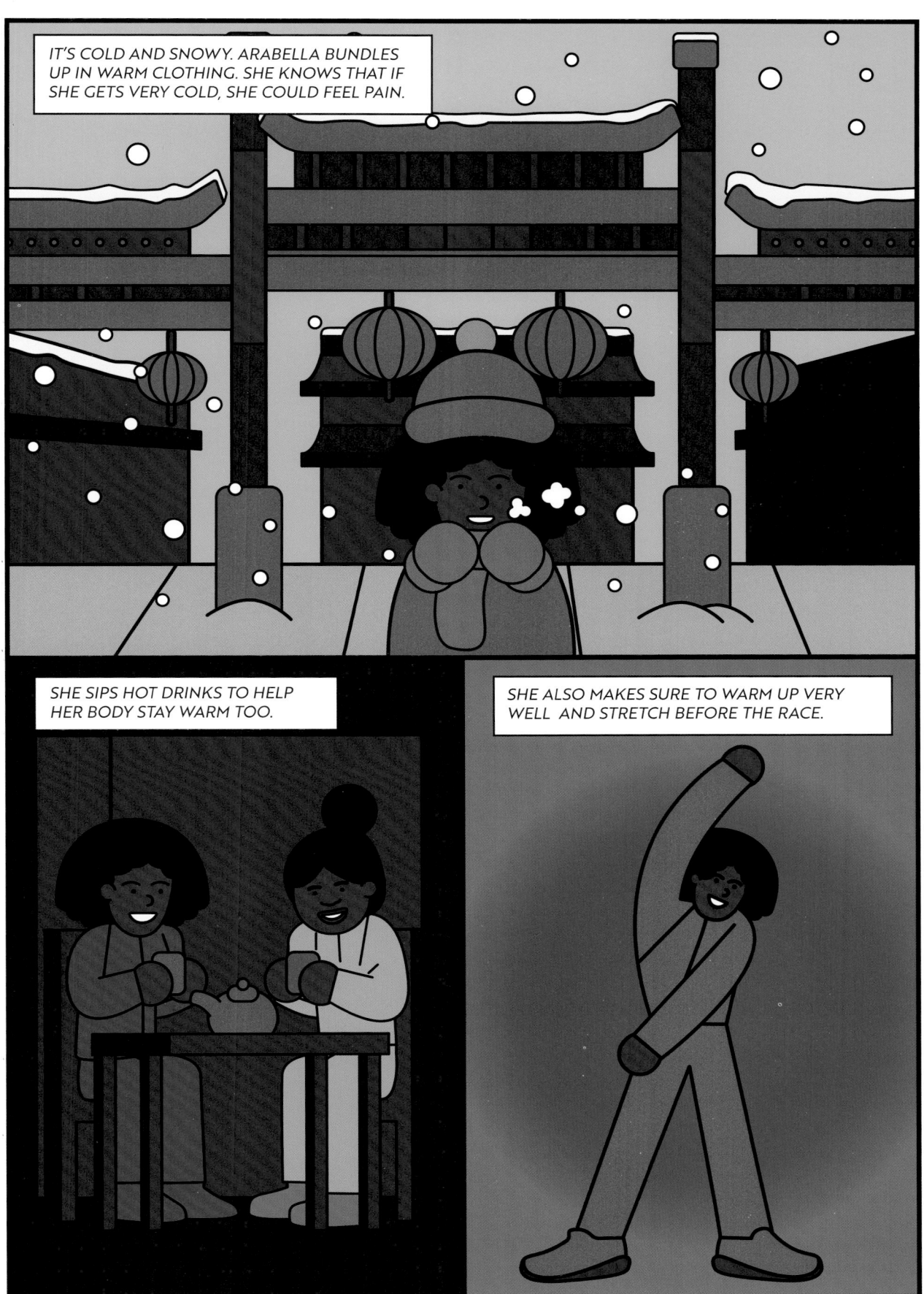

IT'S COLD AND SNOWY. ARABELLA BUNDLES UP IN WARM CLOTHING. SHE KNOWS THAT IF SHE GETS VERY COLD, SHE COULD FEEL PAIN.

SHE SIPS HOT DRINKS TO HELP HER BODY STAY WARM TOO.

SHE ALSO MAKES SURE TO WARM UP VERY WELL AND STRETCH BEFORE THE RACE.

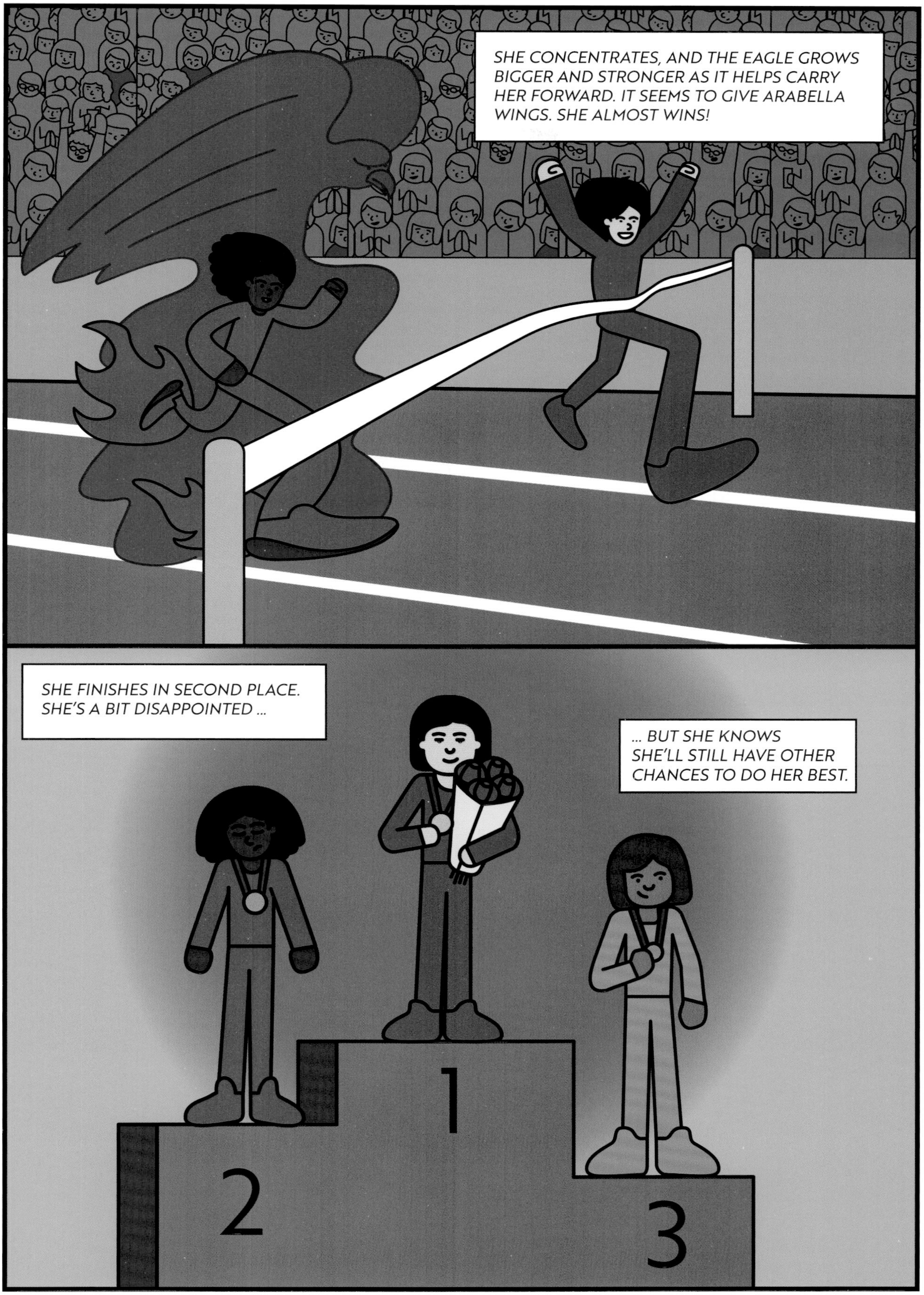
SHE CONCENTRATES, AND THE EAGLE GROWS BIGGER AND STRONGER AS IT HELPS CARRY HER FORWARD. IT SEEMS TO GIVE ARABELLA WINGS. SHE ALMOST WINS!
SHE FINISHES IN SECOND PLACE. SHE'S A BIT DISAPPOINTED ...
... BUT SHE KNOWS SHE'LL STILL HAVE OTHER CHANCES TO DO HER BEST.
1
2
3

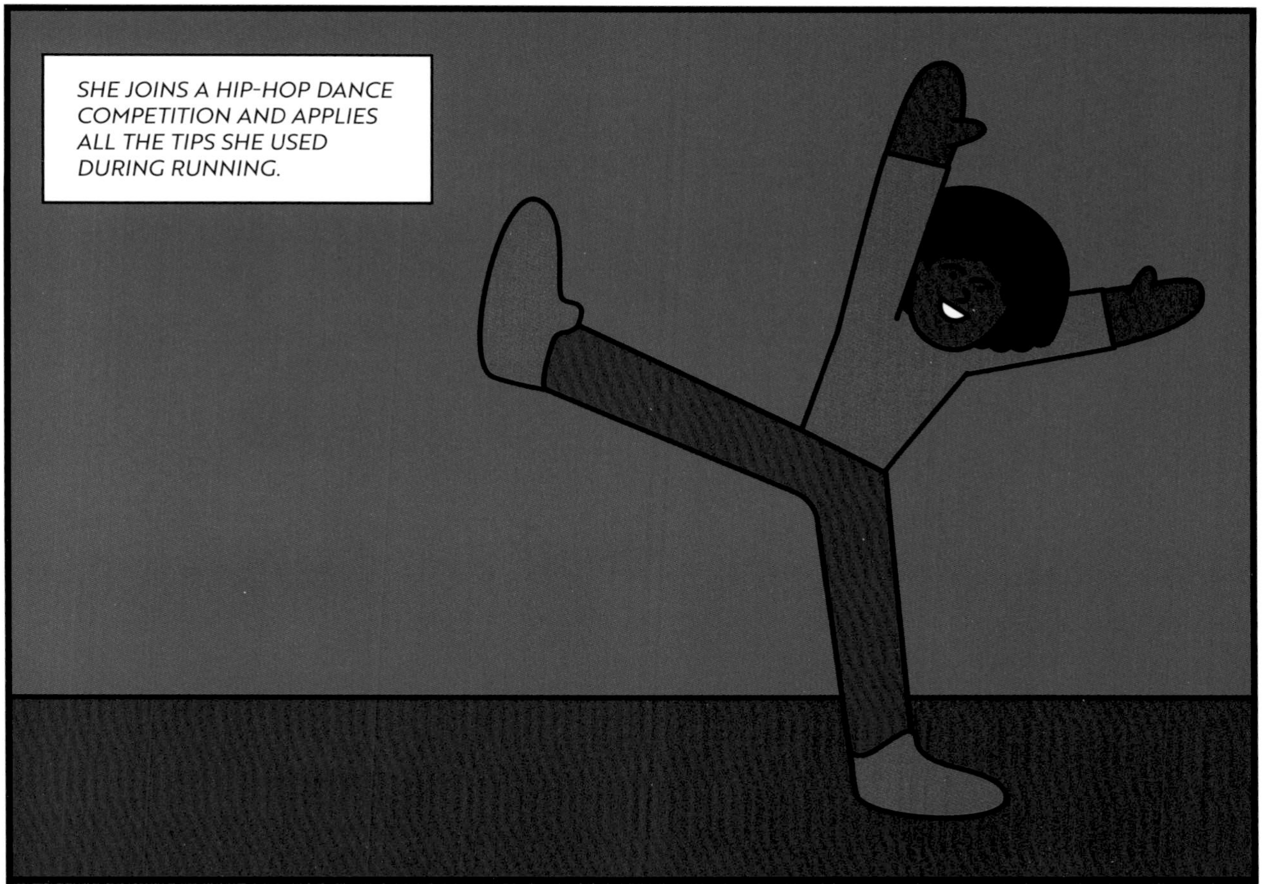
SHE JOINS A HIP-HOP DANCE COMPETITION AND APPLIES ALL THE TIPS SHE USED DURING RUNNING.

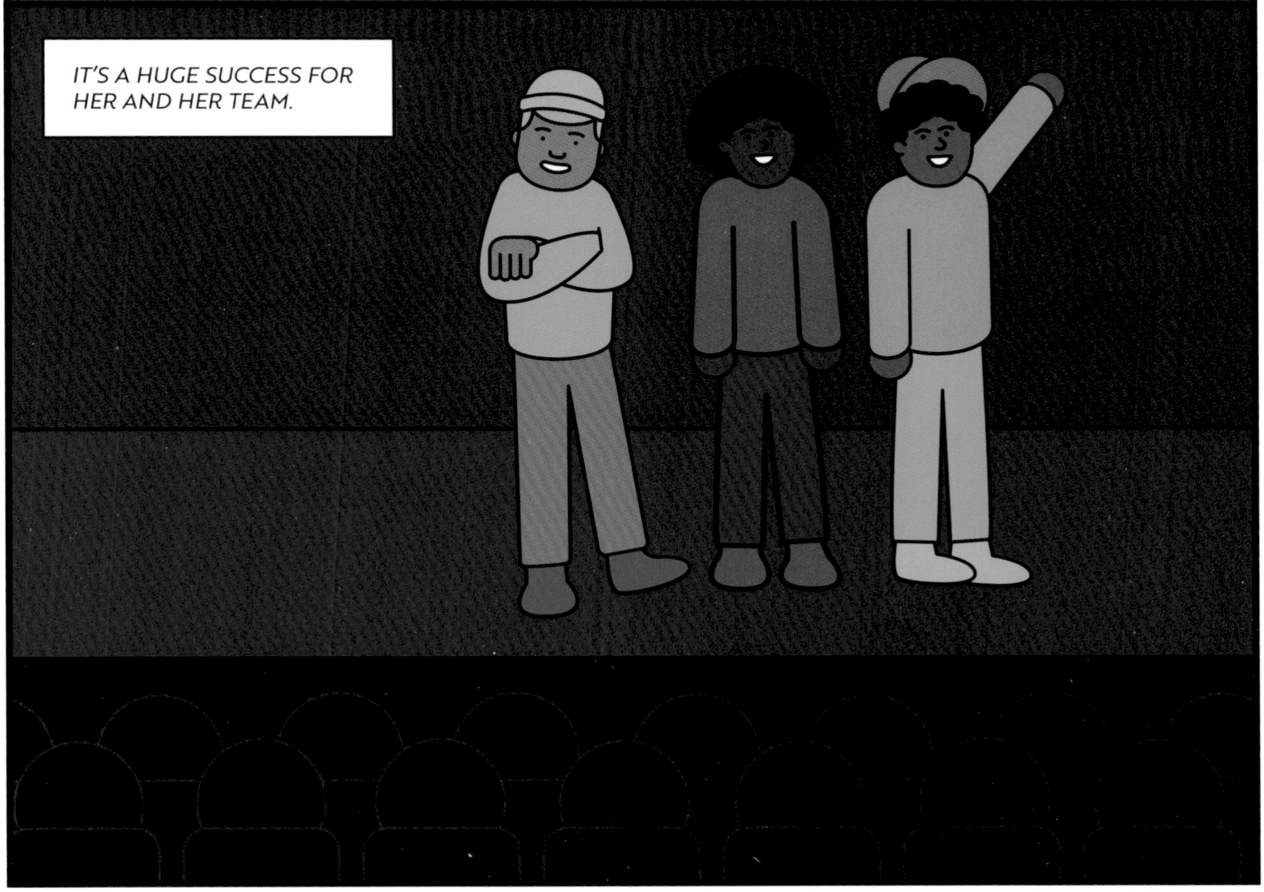
IT'S A HUGE SUCCESS FOR HER AND HER TEAM.

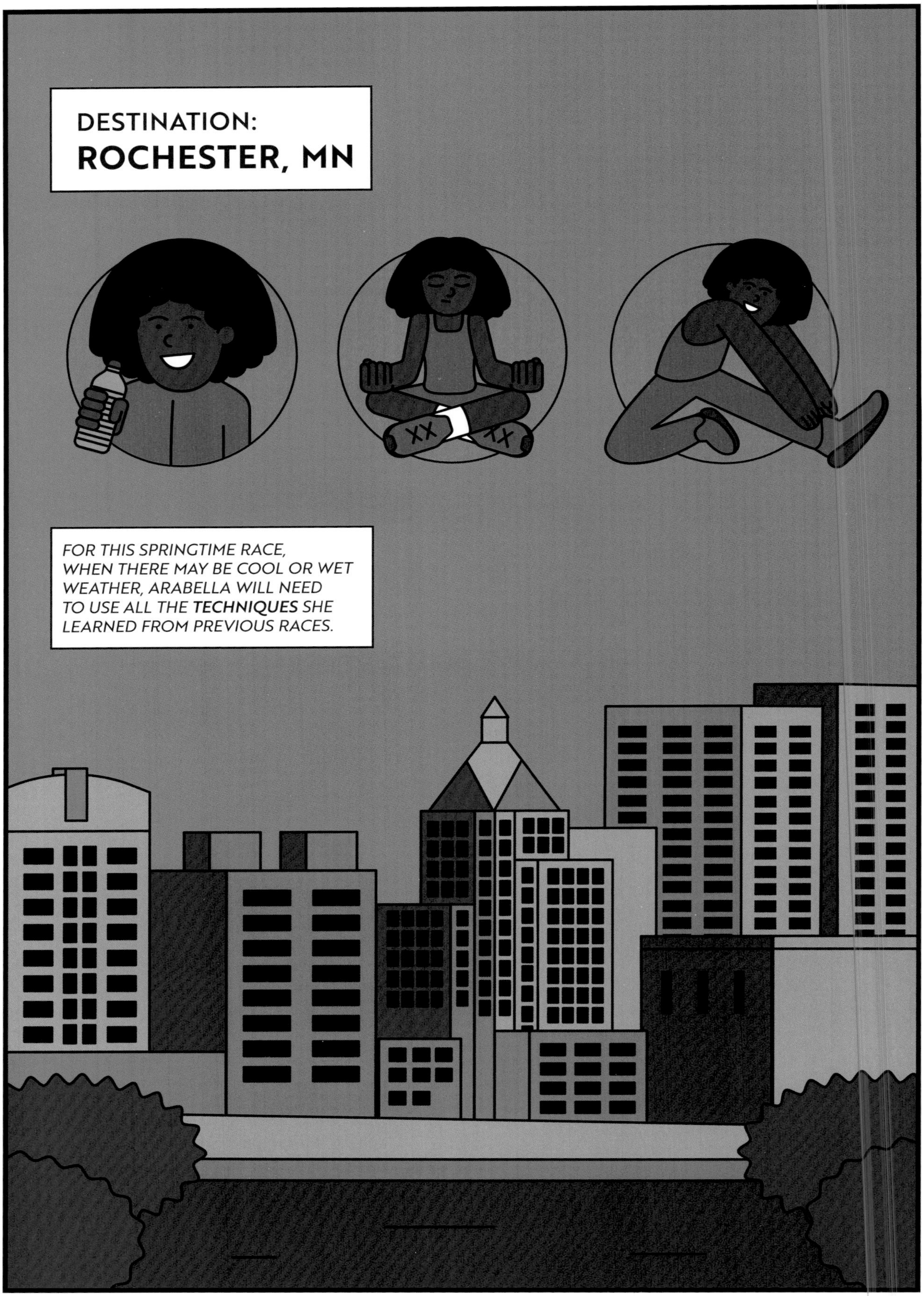
DESTINATION:
ROCHESTER, MN
FOR THIS SPRINGTIME RACE, WHEN THERE MAY BE COOL OR WET WEATHER, ARABELLA WILL NEED TO USE ALL THE **TECHNIQUES** SHE LEARNED FROM PREVIOUS RACES.

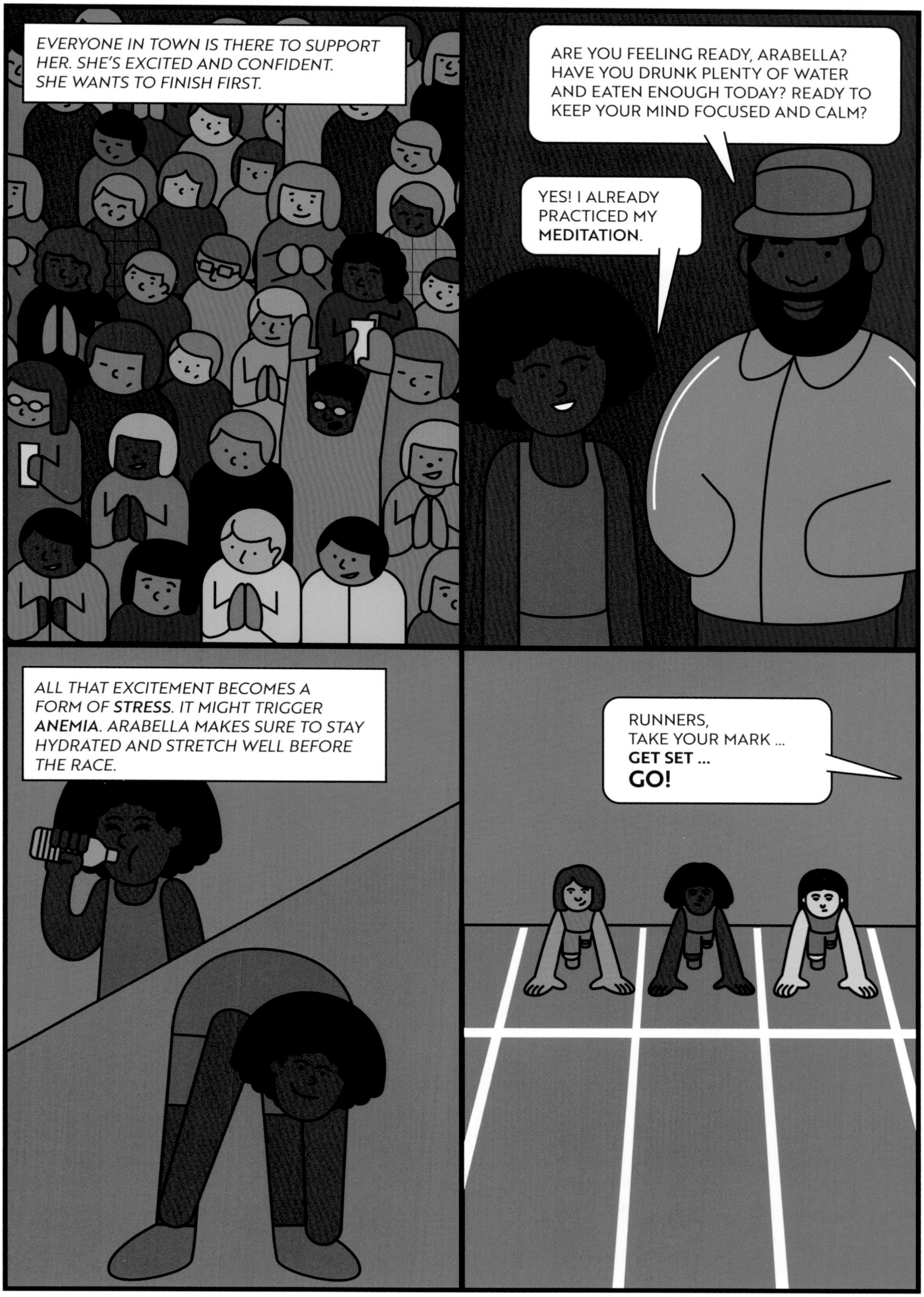
EVERYONE IN TOWN IS THERE TO SUPPORT HER. SHE'S EXCITED AND CONFIDENT. SHE WANTS TO FINISH FIRST.
ARE YOU FEELING READY, ARABELLA? HAVE YOU DRUNK PLENTY OF WATER AND EATEN ENOUGH TODAY? READY TO KEEP YOUR MIND FOCUSED AND CALM?
YES! I ALREADY PRACTICED MY **MEDITATION**.
ALL THAT EXCITEMENT BECOMES A FORM OF **STRESS**. IT MIGHT TRIGGER **ANEMIA**. ARABELLA MAKES SURE TO STAY HYDRATED AND STRETCH WELL BEFORE THE RACE.
RUNNERS, TAKE YOUR MARK ... **GET SET ... GO!**

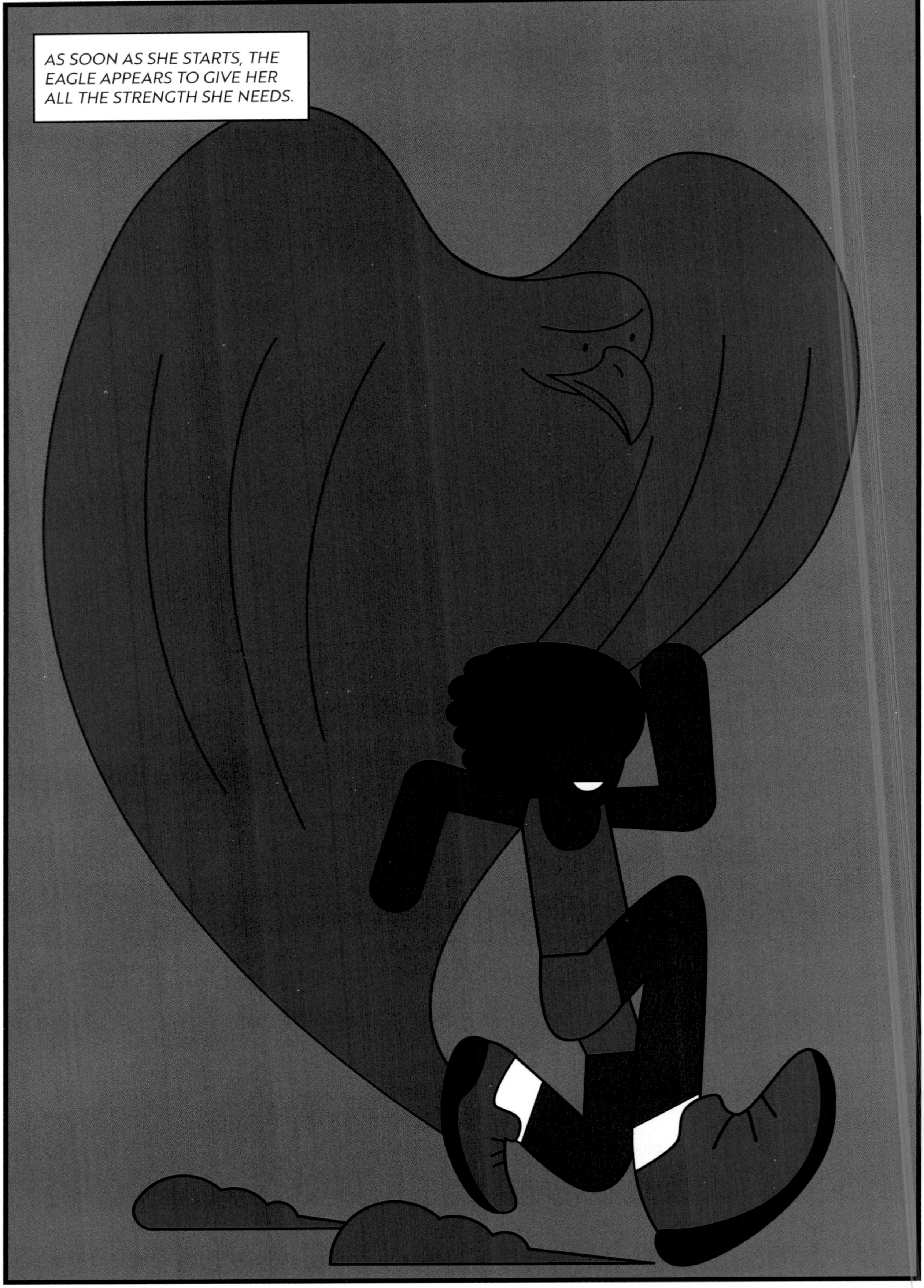
AS SOON AS SHE STARTS, THE EAGLE APPEARS TO GIVE HER ALL THE STRENGTH SHE NEEDS.

ABOUT THE MEDICAL EDITOR

Asmaa Ferdjallah, M.D., M.P.H.
Senior Associate Consultant, Division of Pediatric Hematology/Oncology, Mayo Clinic, Rochester, MN; Assistant Professor of Pediatrics, Mayo Clinic College of Medicine and Science

Dr. Ferdjallah is a pediatric hematologist and bone marrow transplant physician with expertise in sickle cell disease and thalassemia. She envisions a clinical care model where all people with sickle cell disease are cared for by a hematologist with training in bone marrow transplant so that curative therapy can be started sooner. She is also interested in global health, both locally and internationally, and is passionate about optimizing care for people with language or cultural barriers. She strives to set a great example for learners and is passionate about medical education.

ABOUT THE AUTHORS

Guillaume Federighi, aka **Hey Gee**, is a French and American author and illustrator. He began his career in 1998 in Paris, France. He also spent a few decades exploring the world of street art and graffiti in different European capitals. After moving to New York in 2008, he worked with many companies and brands, developing a reputation in graphic design and illustration for his distinctive style of translating complex ideas into simple and timeless visual stories.
He is also the owner and creative director of Hey Gee Studio, a full-service creative agency based in New York City.

Golden Ella was born in Rochester, Minnesota. She enjoys sports, riding her scooter, doing track and field, singing in the honors choir, performing in plays, getting rambunctious with her dog, Samson, and bossing her younger brother around. She became ill at 9 months old and stopped crawling and walking, due to a life-threatening case of osteomyelitis, an infection of the hip and pelvic bones, caused by sickle cell disease. Always a fighter, she worked her way to recovery through surgery, infusions and the medication hydroxyurea. She also credits dedicated care from her health care providers and love and support from her mom, dad, two older sisters, an older brother and a younger brother. She is determined to become a pediatrician focused on hematology and oncology to help other children like her and to find a cure for sickle cell disease.

ABOUT FONDATION IPSEN BOOKLAB

At the service of the general interest, working toward an equitable society, the Fondation Ipsen BookLab publishes and distributes books free of charge, primarily to schools and associations. Through collaborations between experts, artists, authors and children, our publications, for all ages and in a variety of languages, focus on the education and awareness of issues related to health, disability and rare diseases. Discover our complete catalog online at www.fondation-ipsen.org/book-lab.

ABOUT MAYO CLINIC PRESS

Launched in 2019, Mayo Clinic Press shines a light on the most fascinating stories in medicine and empowers individuals with the knowledge to build healthier, happier lives. From the award-winning *Mayo Clinic Health Letter* to books and media covering the scope of human health and wellness, Mayo Clinic Press publications provide readers with reliable and trusted content by some of the world's leading health care professionals. Proceeds benefit important medical research and education at Mayo Clinic. For more information about Mayo Clinic Press, visit MCPress.MayoClinic.org.

ABOUT THE COLLABORATION

The My Life Beyond series was developed in partnership between Fondation Ipsen's BookLab and Mayo Clinic, which has provided world-class medical education for more than 150 years. This collaboration aims to provide trustworthy, impactful resources for understanding childhood diseases and other problems that can affect children's well-being.

The series offers readers a holistic perspective of children's lives with — and beyond — their medical challenges. In creating these books, young people who have been Mayo Clinic patients worked together with author-illustrator Hey Gee, sharing their personal experiences. The resulting fictionalized stories authentically bring to life the patients' emotions and their inspiring responses to challenging circumstances. In addition, Mayo Clinic physicians contributed the latest medical expertise on each topic so that these stories can best help other patients, families and caregivers understand how children perceive and work through their own challenges.

Text: Hey Gee and Golden Ella
Illustrations: Hey Gee

Medical editor: Asmaa Ferdjallah, M.D., M.P.H., Senior Associate Consultant, Division of Pediatric Hematology/Oncology, Mayo Clinic, Rochester, MN; Assistant Professor of Pediatrics, Mayo Clinic College of Medicine and Science

Managing editor: Anna Cavallo, Health Education and Content Services/Mayo Clinic Press, Mayo Clinic, Rochester, MN
Project manager: Kim Chandler, Department of Education, Mayo Clinic, Rochester, MN
Manager of publications: Céline Colombier-Maffre, Fondation Ipsen, Paris, France
President: James A. Levine, M.D., Ph.D., Professor, Fondation Ipsen, Paris, France

MAYO CLINIC PRESS KIDS
200 First St. SW
Rochester, MN 55905
mcpress.mayoclinic.org

ISBN: 978-1-945564-65-9 (HC); 978-1-945564-66-6 (ePub)

Library of Congress Control Number 2022942498

Printed in the United States of America